NATURAL DISASTERS
MEETING THE CHALLENGE

HURRICANE
READINESS

Rachel Seigel

Crabtree Publishing Company

www.crabtreebooks.com

CRABTREE
PUBLISHING COMPANY
WWW.CRABTREEBOOKS.COM

Author: Rachel Seigel

Series research and development:
Janine Deschenes, Reagan Miller

Editorial director: Kathy Middleton

Editors: Ellen Rodger, Melissa Boyce

Proofreader: Wendy Scavuzzo

Design and photo research:
Margaret Amy Salter
Katherine Berti

Prepress technician:
Tammy McGarr

Print and production coordinator:
Katherine Berti

Images:

Alamy Stock Photo
Jim West: p. 41
Suzanne Long: p. 13
cera.coastalrisk.live
Screen Shot 2019-08-16 at
11.08.37 AM: p. 24 (inset)
EON Images: p. 15 (bottom)
Flickr
European Space Agency—
contains modified
Copernicus Sentinel data
(2019), processed by ESA,
CC BY-SA 3.0 IGO: p. 1
Florida International
University: p. 28
Getty Images: Jose Jimenez/
Stringer: p. 5 (bottom)
International Federation of
Red Cross: Paul Grierson:
p. 19
iStockphoto
switas: p. 25
National Oceanic
and Atmospheric
Administration: p 31
VIIRS, captured on SNPP
satellite: p. 18 (top)
Shutterstock
america365: p. 37

ChameleonsEye: p. 18
dennizn: p. 36
Erin Cadigan: p. 22 (both)
Everett Historical:
p. 27 (bottom left)
FashionStock.com:
p. 11 (bottom right)
Joseph Sohm: p. 27 (center)
Mia2you: p. 43
michelmond: p. 40
MiroslavP: p. 12
MISHELLA: p. 10,
11 (bottom left)
SB_photos: p. 34
Terry Kelly: p. 46
Wikimedia Commons
Kelvinsong: p. 6
NASA image by Jeff
Schmaltz, MODIS
Rapid Response Team,
Goddard Space Flight
Center: p. 5 (top)
rheins: p. 13 (top)
Sebastian Ballard:
p. 33 (top)
Timvasquez at English
Wikipedia: p. 20
All other images by
Shutterstock

Library and Archives Canada Cataloguing in Publication

Title: Hurricane readiness / Rachel Seigel.
Names: Seigel, Rachel, author.
Description: Series statement: Natural disasters: meeting the
challenge | Includes bibliographical references and index.
Identifiers: Canadiana (print) 2019013433X |
Canadiana (ebook) 20190134348 |
ISBN 9780778765226 (hardcover) |
ISBN 9780778765288 (softcover) |
ISBN 9781427123800 (HTML)
Subjects: LCSH: Hurricanes—Juvenile literature. |
LCSH: Emergency management—Juvenile literature.
Classification: LCC QC944.2 .S45 2019 | DDC j551.55/2—dc23

Library of Congress Cataloging-in-Publication Data

Names: Seigel, Rachel, author.
Title: Hurricane readiness / Rachel Seigel.
Description: New York : Crabtree Publishing Company, [2020] |
Series: Natural disasters: meeting the challenge |
Includes bibliographical references and index.
Identifiers: LCCN 2019025172 (print) | LCCN 2019025173 (ebook) |
ISBN 9780778765226 (hardcover) |
ISBN 9780778765288 (paperback) | ISBN 9781427123800 (ebook)
Subjects: LCSH: Hurricanes--Juvenile literature. | Hurricane protection--
Juvenile literature. | Emergency management--Juvenile literature.
Classification: LCC QC944.2 .S45 2020 (print) | LCC QC944.2 (ebook) |
DDC 551.55/2--dc23
LC record available at https://lccn.loc.gov/2019025172
LC ebook record available at https://lccn.loc.gov/2019025173

Crabtree Publishing Company

www.crabtreebooks.com   1-800-387-7650

Printed in the U.S.A./102019/CG20190809

**Published
in Canada
Crabtree Publishing**
616 Welland Ave.
St. Catharines, Ontario
L2M 5V6

**Published in the
United States
Crabtree Publishing**
PMB 59051
350 Fifth Avenue, 59th Floor
New York, New York 10118

**Published in the
United Kingdom
Crabtree Publishing**
Maritime House
Basin Road North, Hove
BN41 1WR

**Published
in Australia
Crabtree Publishing**
Unit 3–5 Currumbin Court
Capalaba
QLD 4157

Contents

Hurricanes and Disasters

A tropical cyclone is one of the most powerful and damaging weather systems on Earth. It is a high-speed windstorm that packs a punch with **torrential** rain and an unusually high water level known as a storm surge.

Many Names

Each year, about 80 tropical cyclones form around the world. What they are called depends on where they are from. In the North Atlantic and East Pacific oceans, these tropical cyclones are called hurricanes. In the western North Pacific and the Philippines, they are called typhoons. In the Indian and South Pacific oceans, they are called cyclones.

When **HURRICANES** come onto land, the heavy rain, strong winds, and high water levels can damage buildings, trees, and cars. The high water level is called a **STORM SURGE.**

2018 was one of the busiest hurricane seasons on record. Over a period of 70 days, **22 MAJOR HURRICANES** struck land in the **northern hemisphere**.

Hazards and Vulnerabilities

Tropical cyclone, hurricane, or typhoon—whatever you call them, they are natural hazards. Hazards are threats that can have devastating effects on human populations—especially if we don't plan for them. Hazards can cause disasters that can seriously disrupt how a community or country functions. They have negative effects on people and the environment because of where they happen, how often, how severe they are, and how people cope with them. Some places and communities are more **vulnerable** to disasters, or are more likely to be harmed.

When a natural hazard such as a hurricane affects a human population that is unprepared for it, it can become a disaster. Sometimes, disasters happen because we alter the environment without thinking of the impact. They also happen because communities don't have the money to recover, or even plan for recovery.

*Hurricane Dorian made **landfall** in the Bahamas on September 1, 2019. The hurricane caused widespread destruction and left tens of thousands of people homeless.*

5

Hurricane Seasons

Atlantic Ocean hurricanes have a season between June and November. These hurricanes usually start as storms off the coast of Africa called tropical waves—often just referred to as waves. They progress to large thunderstorms called tropical disturbances when they are about 62 miles (100 km) across. As they grow higher and larger, they are called tropical depressions. Storms with wind speeds of 39 miles per hour (63 kph) or more are labeled tropical storms. When wind speeds hit 74 miles per hour (119 kph) they become tropical cyclones, or hurricanes. Cyclones tend to form in the North Indian Ocean between April and December. Typhoons tend to form in the Pacific between May and October.

1. *Hurricanes form when warm, moist air from the ocean's surface starts to rise quickly, causing an area of low pressure below. When the higher-pressure air meets the lower-pressure air, the new air becomes moist and also rises.*

2. *As warm air keeps rising, air swirls take its place. When the warm, moist air cools off, water in the air forms clouds. The clouds and wind spin and grow, taking energy from the heat and the ocean water **evaporating** from the surface.*

Cross Section of a Hurricane

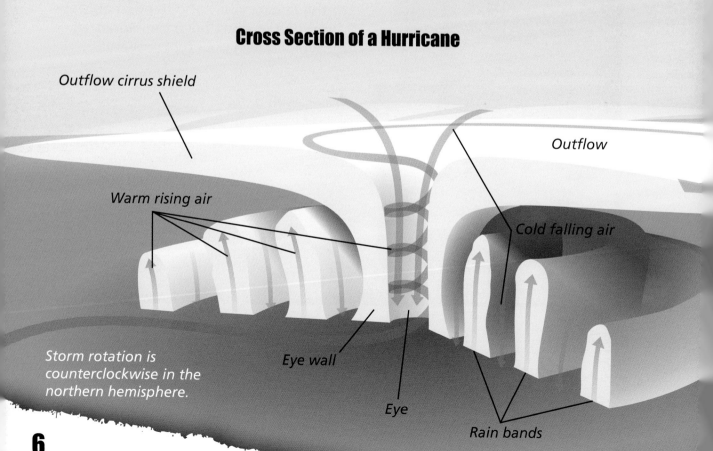

Outflow cirrus shield

Outflow

Warm rising air

Cold falling air

Storm rotation is counterclockwise in the northern hemisphere.

Eye wall

Eye

Rain bands

CASE STUDY
Hurricane Season Lessons Learned

Hurricanes are given names by the **WORLD METEOROLOGICAL ORGANIZATION (WMO)**. Each year, tropical storms are named in alphabetical order. That name stays with the storm if it develops into a hurricane.

Every hurricane season has something to teach both scientists and the public, and important lessons were learned from the 2018 Atlantic hurricane season. Hurricanes Michael and Florence were reminders that it only takes one storm to cause tremendous damage and that **inland** communities as well as coastal communities are at risk from hurricanes. Inland communities need to be better prepared for storms that make landfall and travel. Meteorologists—the weather scientists who track storms and hurricanes—need to communicate the risk to people far from the coast.

Michael was the first Category 5 hurricane to strike the United States since Hurricane Andrew devastated Florida in 1992. Category 5 storms have winds reaching 157 miles per hour (253 kph) or more.

Florence was the first major hurricane of 2018. Florence also proved that just because something happened before, it doesn't mean it will happen the exact same way again. Meteorologists can make a good guess about where a storm will go based on history, but storms are not entirely predictable. No storm following Florence's initial path had ever reached North America before. Meteorologists did a good job of predicting the rain leading up to Florence, but many people focused on the numbering system that categorizes the storm instead. Florence set records for rain in South Carolina and North Carolina and led to flooding.

The most important lesson learned from 2018 was that no matter what the weather forecast says, it is never definite. Storms can suddenly change direction, or quickly become more intense, so people always need to prepare for the unexpected.

CHAPTER 1

The Science Behind Hurricanes

Where Do Hurricanes Form?

Hurricanes form under certain conditions. They need warm, deep water with a temperature of more than 80 degrees Fahrenheit (27 °C). They require an atmosphere that cools rapidly with altitude and low wind shear. Wind shear happens when there is a difference in wind speed and direction over a short distance.

Coriolis Effect

Hurricanes never form at or within 300 miles (500 km) of the equator because of an effect called the Coriolis Effect. The Coriolis Effect is a force that acts on winds because Earth is spinning. At the equator, the force is zero, meaning that there isn't enough force to make the wind rotate.

Hurricanes also don't form far away from the equator because the water temperatures are too cold. Because of this, hurricanes can only form in tropical, or hot and humid, areas.

Area of the equator, where hurricanes cannot form

Tropical areas, where hurricanes can form

Arctic areas, where it is too cold for hurricanes to form

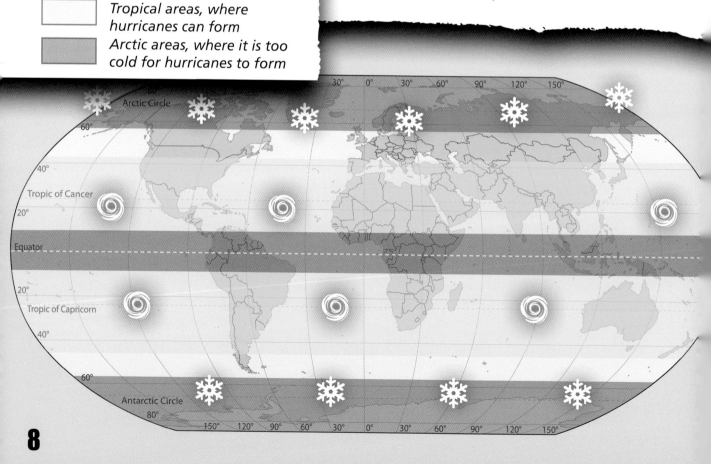

Wind Scale

To estimate the possible damage from a tropical cyclone, scientists use the Saffir-Simpson Hurricane Wind Scale. The scale ranks storms by category from 1–5, based on the continuous wind speed.

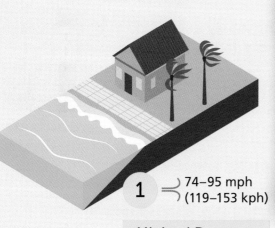

1 74–95 mph (119–153 kph)

Minimal Damage

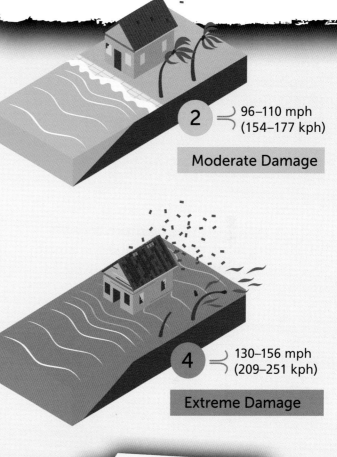

2 96–110 mph (154–177 kph)

Moderate Damage

3 111–129 mph (178–208 kph)

Extensive Damage

4 130–156 mph (209–251 kph)

Extreme Damage

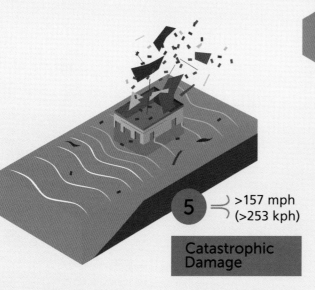

5 >157 mph (>253 kph)

Catastrophic Damage

8.2 FEET (2.5 M)
Hurricane Sandy's storm surge

12 INCHES (30 CM)
Hurricane Sandy's rainfall

$70.2 BILLION
Hurricane Sandy's costs

Rankings

In recent years, many meteorologists say the Saffir-Simpson scale has failed to measure the true destructive strength of storms and a better way of ranking hurricanes is needed. The scale measures wind speed, but does not take into account storm surge. In 2012, Hurricane Isaac was ranked a Category 1, but the storm surge at Shell Beach, Louisiana, was more than 11 feet (3.4 m). The damage from hurricanes Harvey (2017), Katrina (2005), and Sandy (2015) was devastating, but mostly caused by storm surge.

Replacement Scales

Scientists are looking for replacements for the scale that will be more reliable in predicting how much damage the storm will bring. A better option might be to use the newly developed Cyclone Damage Potential Index. It measures wind speed, storm size, length of the storm, and how the wind will move. It predicted that Harvey would be much worse than what the Saffir-Simpson scale measured. A more accurate prediction might have helped cities better prepare for and respond to the damage.

Impact on Humans

Hurricanes have a two-part impact on communities: physical damage to property and **infrastructure**, and harm to humans including injuries, health risks, and loss of life. The physical damage is expensive, and it can take a year or longer for communities to recover. Hurricane Irma caused an estimated $250 billion in damage in the United States and it took parts of Florida almost 20 years to recover after Hurricane Andrew.

Flooded Island

After Hurricane Maria struck Puerto Rico in September 2017, 100 percent of the residents lost power and many people had limited access to food and water. Heavy rains and flash floods from the storm made it worse. Since Puerto Rico is an island, it couldn't be evacuated. An estimated 1,000 people died in events related to the storm, many of which happened after the storm. Many months after the storm, people were still without power, running water, or a reliable way to communicate.

Hurricane Harvey's storm surge flooded houses up to their roofs in Spring, Texas. Some of the severe flood damage caused by Harvey in 2017 happened because the city of Houston, Texas, allowed neighborhoods to be built in areas that were known to be at risk for flooding.

12.5 FEET (3.8 M)
Hurricane Harvey's storm surge

51+ INCHES (130 CM)
Hurricane Harvey's rainfall

$108 BILLION
Hurricane Harvey's costs

Flooding and damage caused by Hurricane Sandy's storm surge

Disaster Planning

After Maria, Puerto Rico's government created a Disaster Recovery Action Plan to outline how it will use disaster relief funds to create better power strategies. Electric power is needed to light the island and to keep hospitals and schools running. One goal for the island is to install solar stand-alone systems with battery backup for emergencies.

10,000 solar power systems were installed in Puerto Rico after Maria.

Vulnerability

Cyclone Idai hit Malawi, Mozambique, and Zimbabwe in southeast Africa in March 2019. It was the worst weather disaster ever to hit the **southern hemisphere**. As of April 2019, the death toll was more than 1,000 people. There were also 4,000 reported cases and seven deaths in Mozambique from cholera, a disease caused by bacteria from drinking water that contains bacteria. The cyclone showed that these poor African countries were particularly vulnerable to such a major storm. **Aid agencies** provided help, but disaster researchers say more resources need to be put into disaster planning to lessen the impact of cyclones and **climate change**. The African Risk Capacity (ARC) agency helps African governments create disaster plans.

In the aftermath of Cyclone Idai, aid agencies delivered food, clean water, shelter, and other basic needs to survivors.

SCIENCE BIO
Urban Flood Management

Researchers from the Institute of Atmospheric Physics in China have a new tool in their hurricane research toolkit: a submarine that shoots research rockets at hurricanes. The institute is part of the Chinese Academy of Sciences. It tested the uncrewed semi-submersible vehicle (USSV) in 2017. The USSV studies the interaction between the air and the sea, and the weather it produces. It was developed to take accurate measurements. The USSV allows scientists to gather information in typhoon weather when **weather balloons** cannot be used. Instead, the USSV can launch sounding, or measuring rockets up to 4,035 feet (1,230 m). These rockets gather real-time data on the air pressure, temperature, wind speed, and direction of typhoons.

Institute of Atmospheric Physics

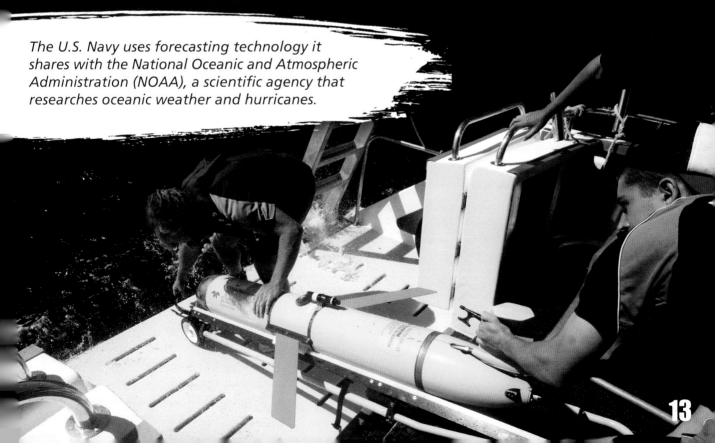

The U.S. Navy uses forecasting technology it shares with the National Oceanic and Atmospheric Administration (NOAA), a scientific agency that researches oceanic weather and hurricanes.

CASE STUDY
Lessons Learned from Katrina

Hurricane Katrina was one of the deadliest and most expensive storms in United States history. It was responsible for the deaths of more than 1,200 people and caused more than $108 billion in damages. The storm uncovered a number of problems that led to Katrina becoming a serious natural disaster.

The main reason that Katrina was so damaging was that the **levees,** which should have protected New Orleans from the storm, failed. This caused major flooding in the city and was responsible for a lot of damage. One year after the storm, a report from the U.S. Army Corps of Engineers found that a lack of proper funding and poor construction led to the levee failures. The U.S. Army Corps of Engineers is the government agency in charge of a number of public works, such as dams and flood protection.

An estimated **400,000 PEOPLE** were permanently displaced from their homes by Katrina.

Unheeded Warnings

For many years before the storm hit, experts had also been warning the city that it was likely to flood. After Katrina, the city learned that it had to make stronger **building codes**. Now homes have to be built at least 3 feet (0.9 m) higher than the level to which floodwaters are expected to rise.

Another big problem during the hurricane was a lack of coordination between government officials, relief organizations, the military, and the Federal Emergency Management Agency (FEMA). FEMA is the part of the government responsible for disaster relief. This lack of coordination left a lot of people waiting for help. FEMA was criticized, but its job was to support the governor of the state, who was in charge of emergency response.

Levees like this one are built to prevent flooding, but the levees that should have protected New Orleans failed.

Since Katrina, state and federal groups bring all of their resources together and work as a team instead of operating individually. The U.S. Congress has also given FEMA more resources that they can use more quickly. FEMA now has the authority to start preparing resources such as food and water before a state governor declares a natural disaster.

Members of the FEMA Urban Search and Rescue Task Force begin their mission to assist residents affected by Hurricane Katrina.

15

CHAPTER 2

Studying Disasters

Several months before the start of each hurricane season, groups of meteorologists make their predictions about how many hurricanes (major and minor) there will be that season. Organizations such as the National Oceanic and Atmospheric Administration (NOAA), Tropical Storm Risk (TSR), Colorado State University's Department of Atmospheric Sciences, and *The Weather Channel* all make predictions for the Atlantic hurricane season. Every season, scientists at the NOAA fly into hurricanes, study observations and models, and think about what kinds of technology can improve their ability to observe hurricanes.

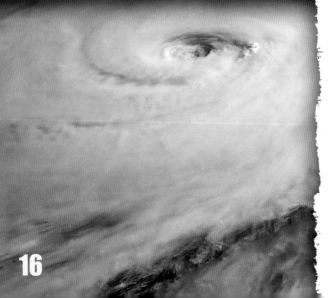

Storm Trackers

These organizations track storms as they develop using modern technology such as satellites, weather **radar**, and computers. Meteorologists use computer programs called numerical weather prediction models. These are mathematical models that predict how a storm is likely to develop. They including intensity, movement, and where and how fast one will make landfall.

Other Technology

There are also many other kinds of technology being used to monitor and study hurricanes. These include:

MICROWAVE IMAGERY

uses the same kind of technology that's in kitchen microwaves. It can give satellites the ability to look inside clouds at multiple layers of a storm. Forecasters use the information to get a better idea of how strong a hurricane is and whether or not it is getting weaker or stronger.

DROPSONDES

(reverse traveling weather balloons) are released by NASA and Air Force Reserve aircraft into and around hurricanes. Dropsondes study wind speed and direction, temperature, moisture content, and **atmospheric pressure**, by collecting **data** all the way down. Some types of dropsondes can even collect data in the oceans. The information that they collect from inside the storms and about the environment around the storms is inserted into computer weather models. These are used to help forecasters be more accurate.

OCEANIC GLIDERS

are underwater robotic gliders that take direct measurements of water temperature and salt content 1,000 feet (305 m) below the water. This helps predict changes in hurricane intensity.

GOES EAST and GOES WEST

are the first two of four new satellites that will let scientists see everything from eastern Australia to western Africa.

GOES WEST

launched in 2018 and can see Pacific hurricanes as far as Hawaii. It can also view typhoons in the western Pacific, and cyclones between Australia and Papua New Guinea. When the second pair launch, they will be the model of weather satellites through 2036.

GOES EAST

stays in one spot, floating above Earth. It captures images of weather and weather systems as frequently as every 30 seconds. This will help meteorologists give earlier and more accurate warnings.

CASE STUDY
Red Cross Disaster Simulation

Tropical Cyclone Winston was the strongest and most intense cyclone on record when it cut through the Pacific islands of Fiji on February 20, 2016. It flattened homes and killed 44 people before fading out over Queensland, Australia.

Just one month before Winston, the Australian Red Cross tested its disaster response skills in a **simulation** exercise. Simulation exercises allow aid and rescue organizations to prepare for real disasters. Sometimes they use actors who pretend they are disaster survivors. They also test disaster plans so that when one happens, people know how to help.

Cyclone Winston reached wind speeds of up to 185 miles per hour (300 kph). Corrugated metal homes such as these ones were no match for the cyclone.

The Australian Red Cross's simulation tested team readiness and response, as well as communications. One goal was to improve cooperation between Red Cross teams located in different areas and countries. When Winston was identified as a threat just weeks later, Red Cross teams in Australia, Fiji, and New Zealand were quickly put on alert.

After Winston hit Fiji, the Red Cross there put plans in motion for **evacuating**, housing, and feeding people. In Australia, the Red Cross was able to notify media that donations were needed to begin reconstruction. That appeal raised more than $1 million. The Australian Red Cross will continue holding disaster simulations to further strengthen their ability to respond to any crisis.

In just **18 MONTHS**, Fiji's Red Cross helped

77,000

people recover from the damage caused by **CYCLONE WINSTON**

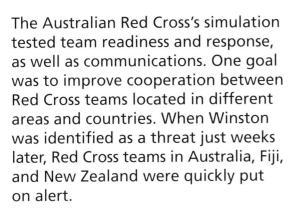

Fiji Red Cross volunteers train to use water purification equipment

Storm Warnings

There are many ways to inform people about the risk of a hurricane, including emergency alerts, news media, and warnings over radio. One of the more current monitoring and warning methods is smartphone and tablet apps. Most of these have animated maps showing the storm's progress. Media websites such as miamiherald.com and the FEMA app warn people about storms and provide real-time information. Weather information channels also have storm radar apps that track hurricanes in incredible detail. Many cities that have emergency management programs send out emails to residents warning of approaching hurricanes. Social media is another well-used warning method. Facebook and Twitter offer options for spreading the word.

Storm Watches

Local weather services work in partnership with the National Disaster Management Authority in India to issue warnings about tropical cyclones and their development. These are broadcast on local television stations or radio stations. Specific forecast information for a particular area can also be found at the National Weather Service at www.weather. gov. A hurricane watch lets people know that a hurricane could develop, but doesn't mean it will happen. A hurricane warning is issued when a hurricane is expected to hit within 36 hours.

*Storm monitoring and warning methods, including storm radar apps, social media, and smart grid technology, play a key role in hurricane **preparedness**.*

7 AM EDT)

Social Media's Broad Reach

When an area is affected by a natural disaster, social media websites such as Facebook and Twitter act as information exchanges. They provide people with information on where to get water and other supplies, helping people in the **aftermath** of a hurricane. After Hurricane Sandy in 2012, people used the Internet and social media to organize relief efforts. After hurricanes Harvey and Irma in 2017, the walkie-talkie app Zello saw an increase in popularity. Rescuers use it to communicate in disaster zones because it can reach people. Users can post voice messages or photos to channels used by rescuers. It demonstrates that people have learned from previous storms that apps can play an important role in emergency preparedness.

Strengthening the Grid

Power companies are also using new technology to strengthen power distribution grids. Grids are the electricity transmission systems that are connected to power lines. Since Hurricane Wilma in 2006, Florida Power & Light has been making improvements to strengthen the grid and make the service more reliable during and after storms. These include smart grid technology and automated switches to find problems and restore service faster. Smart grids are electrical grids that use computers to restore electricity quicker after power outages. Power companies are also using infrared technology to detect problems before they occur. Infrared technology uses invisible light energy to send signals for communication.

Disaster Recovery Strategies

One of the most important parts of disaster recovery is making sure that there is a strategy, or plan, in place for how it will happen. In New Jersey, the state government provided money for rebuilding after Hurricane Sandy, but all building had to be on higher ground. They used a strategy called Build Back Better (BBB) that was intended not just to rebuild but to make the new construction stronger than it was before. BBB was first introduced in 2006 by the **United Nations** for tsunami recovery. It gained widespread use in hurricane disaster recovery because the methods of building lessened the risk of more damage in future hurricanes.

What Does It Mean?

Build Back Better means using better engineering **practices**, building styles, and materials to construct homes and infrastructure in areas more prone to hurricanes and other natural disasters. In some cases, it also means rebuilding quickly so that people who have lost their homes can be housed without years of waiting.

Some **BBB PLANS** ask people who have survived disasters for their ideas on how to rebuild. Rebuilt housing needs to fit how people live and work in a community.

SCIENCE BIO
David Dilley and GWO

David Dilley is a scientist, climatologist, and meteorologist who founded Global Weather Oscillations (GWO), a Florida company that develops technology for climate and weather predictions. His ClimatePulse technology has successfully predicted seven hurricanes to make landfall in the U.S. from 2016 to 2018. The company makes predictions based on the natural cycles of Earth, the Sun, and the moon. ClimatePulse covers 11 zones in the U.S. from New England to Texas.

There are even two prediction zones for the Lesser Antilles, a group of islands in the Caribbean Sea. The predictions tell people what will likely happen in their zone in the upcoming hurricane season. It tells them if the zone will have a hurricane or a tropical storm, where it will make landfall, and with what strength. GWO also works with the International Hurricane Protection Association (INHPA) to help inform citizens and companies about hurricane cycles and prepare for the upcoming season.

CHAPTER 3

Meeting the Challenge

Since 2000, there has been an increase in the number of hurricanes. One reason for the change is that the U.S. is in the midst of an active and dangerous hurricane landfall cycle that occurs every 70 years. Another factor increasing the impact of storms such as Harvey and Irma is climate change. Climate change does not cause the storms, but it makes the results, such as flooding, and wind damage, worse. There is a link between the rising temperatures worldwide and the increase in the strength of these storms.

Hurricane Fuel

Hurricanes are fueled by warm water at the ocean surface. As ocean temperatures increase, the number of storms increases. The warmer temperatures also cause the **ice sheets** and other glaciers to melt, sending more water to the oceans. This makes the sea levels rise, causing more coastal flooding during storms.

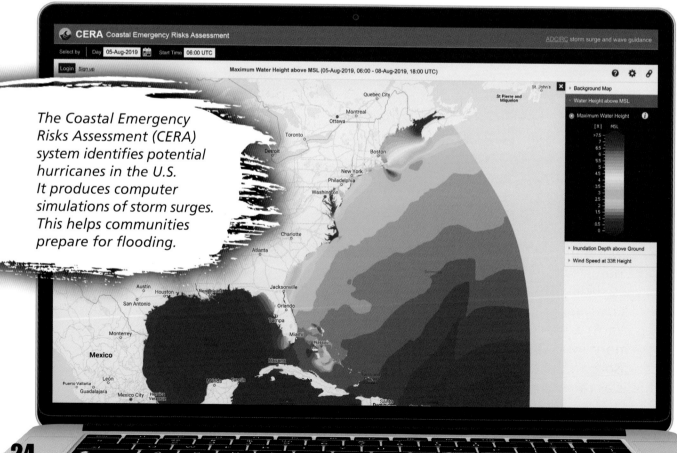

The Coastal Emergency Risks Assessment (CERA) system identifies potential hurricanes in the U.S. It produces computer simulations of storm surges. This helps communities prepare for flooding.

Around the world, **THREE TIMES** as many people are living in houses threatened by hurricanes than there were in **1970.**

Rising Sea Levels

Along the Texas Gulf Coast, sea levels have risen by more than 6 inches (15 cm) in the past few decades. This means that the storm surge caused by Hurricane Harvey in 2018 was 6 inches (15 cm) higher than it would have been in the 1990s. Storm strength is also affected by things such as warmer water. Warm water makes wind speeds more intense. It allows the air to absorb more water, which in turn falls as rain. More moisture also makes heavier rainfalls more likely and increases the chances of flooding.

Human Impact

Population growth and housing development patterns also increase the number of homes that could be affected by hurricanes. In Houston, Texas, for example, the population has grown by 1.8 million people since 2000. That's more people in the storm's path and more homes that could be destroyed or flooded. The growth has led to urban sprawl, or the expansion of city areas into surrounding, formerly rural or country, areas. This means natural areas where rainfall can seep into the soil have been paved over with concrete and asphalt. Water runs off paved surfaces and collects in gutters, drains, and storm sewers. When there is too much rain, the sewers cannot handle the volume, and these neighborhoods and their homes become flooded.

At Hurricane Harvey's peak, one-third of Houston was under water.

Reactive vs Proactive

In the past 25 years, more than 50 percent of the coastal prairie wetlands near Houston, Texas, have been paved over with roads, bridges, and buildings. These wetlands are natural flood barriers that help protect against floods. Since 2010, 8,600 buildings have been built in Harris County, an area that includes Houston, on land that is predicted to flood during a major storm. The city is at great risk of devastating flooding, but experts say city officials have not made building codes stricter.

Public Projects

To withstand hurricanes, cities have to **integrate** with nature and plan for the future. In 2019, voters in Harris County approved a $2.5 billion flood infrastructure bond that will be used to protect against flooding from hurricanes. An infrastructure bond is a way of raising or borrowing money to pay for needed services and projects. Harris County's bond will buy floodplain land and keep it as floodplains. It will also pay for flood channel and detention basins, floodplain mapping, and early flood warning systems. The bond proposal had 85 percent support among voters. This means people in and around Houston want their government to invest in flood protection for all.

To withstand natural disasters such as hurricanes, cities need to integrate their infrastructure with nature.

Lessening Hurricane Impact

When Hurricane Andrew tore through Florida in August 1992, it became the costliest hurricane in the United States with $25.3 billion in damages. In 2005, Hurricane Katrina and Hurricane Harvey topped that figure at $125 billion in damages. There's no doubt that hurricanes are violent and expensive to recover from. One way of lessening the financial impact of hurricanes is to invest in construction that can resist hurricane winds.

An aerial view of damage caused by Hurricane Andrew

HURRICANE CAROL in 1953 was the first "named storm" in the Atlantic to reach **CATEGORY 5** status. There were plenty of Category 5 hurricanes before Carol, but they were named for where they did the most damage, such as the **GREAT NEW ENGLAND HURRICANE OF 1938.**

A house tipped over by storm surge during the Galveston Hurricane of 1900. Also known as the Great Storm of 1900, it was the deadliest natural disaster in United States history. A storm surge of 8 to 12 feet (2.4–3.7 m) swamped the coast and more than 8,000 people died.

CASE STUDY
Florida International University's Wall of Wind

Florida International University's International Hurricane Research Center (IHRC) in Miami is a research and education organization that searches for solutions to lessen the danger of hurricanes. Center researchers work on projects such as hurricane storm surge forecasting and the economic and social costs of hurricanes.

The center's $8 million wall of wind (WoW) tests everything from nails and shingles for roofs to rooftop air conditioning units. The goal is to see how they hold up against hurricane winds. The wall of wind research project began in 2005 as a wind simulator to help test building construction and products. The first WoW was a mobile prototype with two gas-powered fans. The WoW could generate 120-mile-per-hour (193 kph) winds. It had a water-injection system that could simulate the horizontal rain of a hurricane.

The system was developed after Hurricane Andrew to test and improve building designs and materials that had failed during Andrew. Today's WoW is capable of reaching Category 5 level winds of 157 miles per hour (253 kph) or more. It tests the products that are supposedly hurricane resistant to see if they hold up. These include windows and doors, but also transportation structures such as traffic signals, road signs, and bridges. The WoW is computer monitored and tests can be repeated to see if they get the same results. Computer simulations will never be exactly like the real thing, but they can come close.

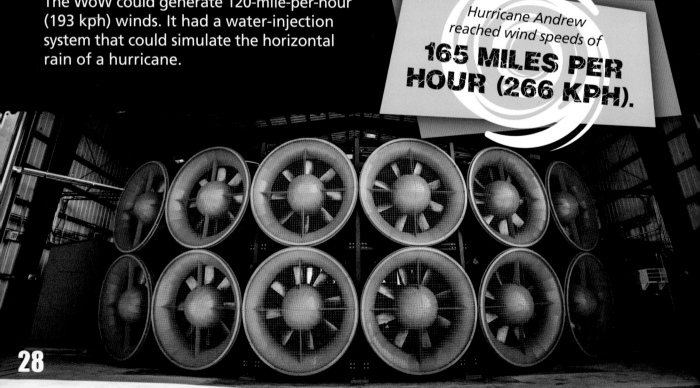

Hurricane Andrew reached wind speeds of **165 MILES PER HOUR (266 KPH).**

Cooling a Hurricane's Fuel

In Norway, scientists have tested a method called a bubble curtain that they hope will lower water temperature and lessen the "fuel power" of a hurricane. The curtain supplies bubbles of compressed air from a pipe with holes that is lowered into the water about 328–492 feet (100–150 m) deep. The bubbles rise, taking with them colder water from deep in the ocean. The cold water mixes with the warmer water at the surface, cooling the warm surface water. The cooler water causes the hurricane to lose its fuel and make a storm less damaging.

In 2017, during hurricanes Harvey, Irma, and Maria, the ocean surface temperatures in the Gulf of Mexico reached 90 degrees Fahrenheit (32 °C), which is what made them so damaging. If the water could have been cooled to below 80 degrees Fahrenheit (26.5 °C), it might have stopped them at the tropical storm stage.

Oil Spill Technology

This bubble curtain technology has already been used to contain oil spills and could be installed on oil rigs. There are already 4,000 oil rigs in the Gulf of Mexico and the technology could be used on a large scale. It would reduce the damage from hurricanes, preventing deaths and saving money over time.

This method won't stop hurricanes, but it can prevent them from getting as intense. It's used in Norway to keep inlets free of ice. Now it's being studied to see how it could be applied around the world.

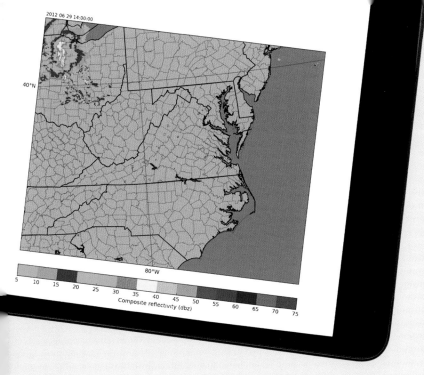

New Tracking Methods

New methods of tracking hurricanes are being developed and tested regularly. A process named Finite-Volume Cubed-Sphere Dynamical Core (FV3) allows scientists to create individual 3-D cubes of data, or information, about a hurricane. It not only tracks speed and wind direction, but also tracks **updrafts** and precipitation. The more data scientists get, the better able they will be to develop reliable systems for tracking hurricanes.

Tracking and prediction systems such as FV3 are being developed for more detailed global weather prediction. FV3 started as a climate-modeling system and was later updated to be more accurate.

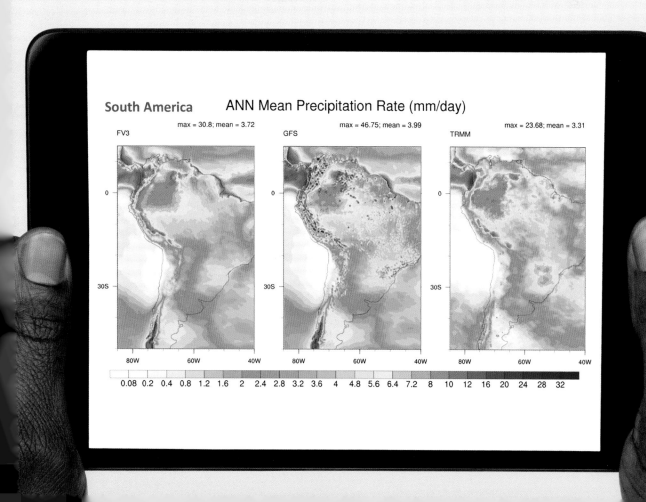

CHAPTER 4

Facing Future Disasters

There is no known way to do anything about the pressure changes that happen as the air rises and cools during a hurricane. Scientists also cannot change the winds. But there are things that communities can do to minimize the impact of a storm.

Living Shorelines

One strategy for lessening storm strength is to create a living shoreline. Living shorelines use plants and other natural elements such as oyster reefs, oyster shells, rocks, and marsh plants. America's Water Infrastructure Act of 2018 is a law that requires the U.S. Army Corps of Engineers to consider using solutions such as living shoreline in combination with engineered structures such as seawalls to protect coastal areas. During Hurricane Florence in 2017, areas with living shorelines suffered less damage than areas that only had seawalls.

Seawalls

Seawalls are hard structures that are designed to block waves as they approach the shore, but they have faults. Not only are they expensive, but when waves hit the seawall, they dig away at the sand at the base. Eventually, a gap grows under the wall. The gap will cause the seawall to crack and tip over.

A living shoreline that uses rocks in combination with a human-made seawall

Growing in Number

While they won't totally prevent the devastating impacts of hurricanes, living shorelines help lessen some of the effects and help communities bounce back faster. As of June 2019, there were more than 120 living shorelines around the U.S. which are effective and less expensive alternatives to seawalls.

Overtopping

High waves can also climb over seawalls and cause flooding. A new type of seawall shaped like a wave is better than vertical seawalls at reflecting waves. However, these walls are more expensive and need to be repaired more often.

Living shorelines can protect the ground from **erosion**, improve the water quality, and make the shoreline more stable over time. Creating or improving salt marshes and wetlands also reduces the storm surge risk to humans and properties. These areas act like sponges, absorbing up to 50 percent of the energy from waves.

Wave-shaped seawall

Future Building Construction

Changes to the construction and design of buildings can also minimize the impact that hurricanes have on homes and other structures. A company in North Carolina is experimenting with building shapes to **deflect** winds. They build circular homes with cone-shaped roofs. This lowers the force of the winds by directing them over and around the building. Architects also have ideas for structures that are secured to the ground, but float up and down on posts.

The dome house on Caxambas Island, Florida, survived Hurricane Andrew in 1992 without much damage because of its rounded structure and elevated footings. Rising sea levels, disrepair, and Hurricane Wilma in 2015, eroded the island and damaged the foundation.

foam

foam

concrete

Homes built from concrete can withstand the high winds of a hurricane better than homes built from wood.

Concrete Construction

Building homes from concrete is another way that they could resist multiple types of disasters. The structure would be built by pouring concrete between stacked foam blocks. It's stronger than wood, but also more expensive.

Green Rooftops

Research shows green rooftops can **absorb** more water. They use plants that absorb the water before it gets funneled into barrels, rather than waiting until it runs down into the street. In New Orleans, there are now seven rain gardens. These are parks where water pools and is absorbed. Creating new green areas in cities will help draw away water that would flood streets and homes.

Green rooftops, like this one in Sydney, Australia, can absorb water, which helps to prevent flooding.

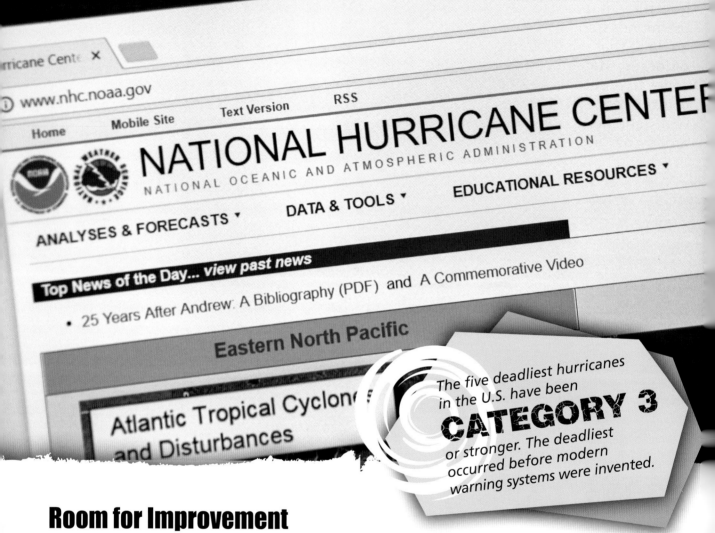

Tropical cyclone activity is not e[xpected]
during the next 48 hours

rricane Cente ×

ⓘ www.nhc.noaa.gov

Home   Mobile Site   Text Version   RSS

NATIONAL HURRICANE CENTER
NATIONAL OCEANIC AND ATMOSPHERIC ADMINISTRATION

ANALYSES & FORECASTS ▾   DATA & TOOLS ▾   EDUCATIONAL RESOURCES ▾

Top News of the Day... view past news

- 25 Years After Andrew: A Bibliography (PDF) and A Commemorative Video

Eastern North Pacific

Atlantic Tropical Cyclone[s] and Disturbances

The five deadliest hurricanes in the U.S. have been **CATEGORY 3** or stronger. The deadliest occurred before modern warning systems were invented.

Room for Improvement

No matter how well a city prepares for a hurricane, each storm shows areas that need improvement. One area of hurricane readiness that needs constant monitoring for improvement is communications. The U.S. government uses weather alert systems such as the emergency alert system (EAS) to send out mass notifications of hurricanes. The EAS sends alerts and warnings through radio, television, and cell phones. The National Hurricane Center also posts advisories on its website, along with maps of hurricanes and storms so that people can visually track them. In Canada, weather warnings and hurricane-tracking information appears on the government's Natural Resources Canada website. Storm alerts are also sent out through the emergency broadcast system on radio and television.

Building Codes

Living in a hurricane-prone area is a risk—both physically and to property. One way to manage that risk is to live in a hurricane-proof home. In the U.S., the federal government has tried to push builders to use higher standards, but building codes are laws that are often the responsibility of local or state governments. Changing codes to ensure that new buildings are constructed with materials that can withstand hurricane winds can save lives and money in insurance claims.

Florida has some of the strongest codes in the U.S. They were set after Hurricane Andrew destroyed more than 125,000 homes and 80,000 businesses in 1992. The state created the Florida Building Code in 2001. Since then, statistics show homes built to Florida Building Code standards suffered 53 percent less damage than homes built before the codes were set.

Some builders oppose stronger building codes because using hurricane-proof building materials increases the construction costs, making it more difficult for them to make money.

Hurricane-Proof Homes

Architects and engineers have designed more effective protections against extreme weather, but many homebuilders have been slow to adapt. Part of the reason is that many people don't know they exist so they don't ask for them. Another big reason is that the new, stronger homes are more expensive, and it is mostly wealthy people who can afford them.

Planning for Hurricanes

The Federal Alliance for Safe Homes (FLASH) is a nonprofit organization in the U.S. that educates and advocates for disaster safety. FLASH follows a model that encourages communities and families to protect their homes and themselves from hurricanes. Their #hurricanestrong program is an effort to help people prepare for hurricanes through pre-planning evacuation routes, building disaster supply kits, strengthening their homes, and helping neighbors. Their website at www.flash. org has a section for kids with hurricane safety and preparation videos.

FLASH recommends that a disaster supply kit includes items such as a flashlight, batteries, **nonperishable** food, and water. For a complete list of items, check out their website at **FLASH.ORG**

SCIENCE BIO
Mark Jacobson and Cristina Archer

Stanford University professor Mark Jacobson and environmental engineer Cristina Archer study how offshore **wind farms** could be used to protect coastlines from approaching hurricanes. Using a computer model to simulate three of the most powerful and destructive hurricanes in recent years, they found that **wind turbines** could reduce hurricane wind speeds—if they were closely spaced.

Jacobson and Archer examined hurricanes Sandy (2012), Katrina (2005), and Isaac (2012) with their computer model, running simulations of giant offshore windfarms strung across the path of the storm. Their simulations found that the presence of closely spaced wind turbines reduced the wind speed of hurricanes up to 50 percent. In addition, they reduced storm surge by 60 to 79 percent. That's a significant change! The simulations also showed hurricanes dissolved much faster once they make landfall— fast enough not to cause damage to wind turbines.

Archer used the weather forecasting model with Hurricane Harvey (2017) as an example. She found that rainfall could be reduced by more than 20 percent, thereby reducing hurricane damage. The Katrina simulation used 78,000 turbines. Currently, the largest wind farm has 7,000 turbines. Archer thinks installing more for a real-life test would be expensive, but would save money by reducing wind damage.

Wind turbines

CASE STUDY
Resources and Reconstruction

In Texas, recovery from Hurricane Harvey has been quicker in wealthier areas partly because people in those communities could rely on insurance and their own savings to pay for their living expenses while their homes were repaired. They were also able to access more in government disaster relief and recovery funds because of the way the government calculated payments for damage.

An estimated **204,000 HOMES** were damaged or destroyed by the flooding caused by Harvey.

Since individuals and communities face disaster risks together, it makes sense to band together and build community resilience.

The state's long-term recovery plan didn't allow for damage of less than $8,000 for homeowners and $2,000 for renters. Housing organization Texas Housers analyzed the numbers and determined that low-income people who owned houses suffered an average of $7,000 in damage. This meant many received no help. Higher-income homeowners suffered damages of $13,500 on average. Lower-income homeowners were also less likely to have insurance that covered all their losses.

A survey done by the Episcopal Health Foundation and the Kaiser Family Foundation found that 30 percent of people who suffered home damage due to Harvey were still not "back to normal" a full year after the hurricane. Most of those were people with lower incomes.

A full 50 percent of lower-income survey respondents said they were not getting the help they needed to recover. By comparison, 32 percent of respondents with higher incomes said they were not getting help.

Groups such as Texas Housers, a low-income housing information service, have been helping people get the funds they need to repair their homes. Texas Housers notes that rebuilding funds are not distributed equally. One way of improving equality is for communities to band together and make community action plans for future disasters. With the idea that many voices are stronger than one, community action plans will help people organize and press for action together instead of separately.

CHAPTER 5

Building Resilience

Today, we can be much more prepared for hurricanes than we ever have been. And scientists are looking for new and improved ways to slow down a hurricane, or to change its path so that it's less destructive. New technologies help forecasters to predict hurricanes much earlier, giving people information during and after the disaster to aid with recovery. Although it is impossible to prevent a hurricane from happening, we can learn from the experiences of past hurricanes. In doing so, we gain a better understanding of how to handle future disasters and how to better protect people from their impact.

Ask Yourself This

Based on the information in this book, what are some of the ways in which humans have learned from hurricanes and their damaging effects over the years?

1. Do you think the world is better prepared for hurricanes than they were 50, or even 20, years ago? Why or why not?

2. What kinds of technology help scientists identify hurricanes?

3. What can people do to try to minimize the destruction of natural disasters such as hurricanes?

4. How does early prediction of hurricanes help save lives?

Bibliography

Introduction

Allen, Greg. "After Hurricane Michael, A Call For Stricter Building Codes In Florida's Panhandle." *NPR*, October 17, 2018. https://n.pr/2EtXyzp

Bell, Samantha S. Detecting Hurricanes. Mendota Heights, MN: North Star Editions, 2017.

"Hurricane Scientists Bring a New Wave of Technology to Improve Forecasts." Atlantic Oceanographic and Meteorological Laboratory. https://bit.ly/2N5VMHt

Stillman, Dan. "What Are Hurricanes?" NASA, August 7, 2017. https://go.nasa.gov/2A73aJX

Chapter 1

Buckland, Tim. "HURRICANE FLORENCE: Lessons learned from the storm." *Star News Online*, October 1, 2018. https://bit.ly/2N4k3xq

"Hurricane Florence Case Study." Internet Geography. https://bit.ly/2KAlUbB

"Hurricane Michael Case Study." Internet Geography. https://bit.ly/31HUg2i

Lott, Melissa C. "Wind turbines could reduce damage from hurricanes without breaking themselves." *Scientific American*, March 12, 2014. https://bit.ly/2OWv7PO

Milford, Lewis M. "As Hurricane Michael damages the Southeast, Puerto Rico provides lessons on resilient power." Brookings, October 12, 2018. https://brook.gs/33uhJ8H

"Official Hurricane Warning Systems." CDEMA, 2010. https://bit.ly/2N6lziy

Precise Consultants. "Can Wind Farms Actually Weaken Hurricanes?" OilPrice.com. October 24, 2018. https://bit.ly/2z11S3w

"Storm Surge Overview." National Hurricane Center and Central Pacific Hurricane Center. www.nhc.noaa.gov/surge

Vick, Karl. "In Puerto Rico, Many of the 3,000 Deaths Were Slow and Painful. Just like the Recovery." *TIME Magazine*, September 20, 2018. http://time.com/longform/hurricane-maria-lessons

Chapter 2

Baron, Sharon Aron. "In Preparation for Hurricane Season, FPL Continues Improvements in Coral Springs." Coral Springs Talk, April 22, 2019. https://bit.ly/2HagBxD

"FAQs - Tropical Cyclones." World Meteorological Organization. https://bit.ly/2vKE3hn

"How They Are Named: differently in different parts of the world." WW2010, University of Illinois. https://bit.ly/2YTmjyP

"Hurricane and Tropical Storm Watches, Warnings, Advisories and Outlooks." National Weather Service. www.weather.gov/safety/hurricane-ww

Mersereau, Dennis. "The 2018 hurricane season taught us some important lessons–so let's not forget them." *Popular Science*, December 5, 2018. https://bit.ly/2Tz4b7n

"Numerical Weather Prediction: forecast models." WW2010, University of Illinois. https://bit.ly/2H9nlMh

Robinson, Caragh, Catherine Harris, Steve Ray, and Ian Morrison. "Case study: How a disaster simulation helped Red Cross prepare for Cyclone Winston." Australian Disaster Resilience Knowledge Hub. https://bit.ly/2YTml9V

Chapter 3

Belles, Jonathan."Six Tools Used to Monitor Hurricanes You've Probably Never Heard Of." *The Weather Channel*, June 19, 2018. https://wxch.nl/2yZJqbt

Connor, Anne N. "Why you want oysters and a salt marsh between you and a hurricane." *Vox*, June 3, 2019. http://bit.ly/2KKRJNO

Dengler, Roni. "Two Studies Confirm That Human Activities Are Making Storms Worse—D-brief." Discover, November 14, 2018. http://bit.ly/2OX0JF7

Gibbens, Sarah. "2018's deadly hurricane season, visualized." *National Geographic*, December 20, 2018. https://on.natgeo.com/2rOvnly

"How do Hurricanes Form?" Precipitation Education, NASA. https://go.nasa.gov/2TGEgJb

Katerere, Yemi. "Lessons from Cyclone Idai." World Wildlife Fund, May 2, 2019. http://bit.ly/2YQwN1D

Kotecki, Peter. "Natural disasters set records around the world in 2018. These were some of the worst." *Business Insider*, December 6, 2018. https://bit.ly/303lDU5

"Lessons learned from Hurricane Sandy." Better World Solutions. https://bit.ly/305XVX1

Mandelbaum, Ryan F. "Chinese Scientists Launch Weather Rocket From Semi-Submersible Vehicle for Typhoon Measurements." Gizmodo. February 1, 2019. https://bit.ly/2KLFu3H

"Natural hazards and disaster risk reduction." World Meteorological Organization. https://bit.ly/33B8PGv

Ramsay, Hamish. "The Global Climatology of Tropical Cyclones." Natural Hazard Science, May 2017. https://bit.ly/2N559qD

Snøfugl, Ingvil. "Preventing hurricanes using air bubbles." SINTEF, March 19, 2018. https://bit.ly/2Tz4m2A

Chapter 4

Appell, David. "We Need a Better Way to Measure Hurricanes." *Slate Magazine*, September 21, 2017. https://bit.ly/2HmjI5N

Associated Press. "Hurricane Irma Death Toll Increased to 129 in U.S., Caribbean after Release of NHC Report." *The Weather Channel*, March 13, 2018. https://wxch.nl/31DSKy2

Block, Deborah. "Lessons Learned From Katrina, 10 Years Later." *VOA News*. August 27, 2015. http://bit.ly/2TAPuAB

Bloomberg. "Hurricane-Proof Homes Exist — Why Isn't Anyone Buying Them?" *Fortune*, June 20, 2018. http://fortune.com/2018/06/20/hurricane-proof-homes

Fernandez, Manny. "A Year After Hurricane Harvey, Houston's Poorest Neighborhoods Are Slowest to Recover." *The New York Times*, September 3, 2018. www.nytimes.com/2018/09/03/us/hurricane-harvey-houston.html

Gibbens, Sarah. "Hurricane Katrina, explained." *National Geographic*, January 16, 2019. https://on.natgeo.com/2H99O7h

Holley, Peter. "Researchers say this technology could be the key to people taking hurricane warnings seriously." *The Washington Post*, October 10, 2018. https://wapo.st/2KLuIdO

Kitchen, Patricia. "Hofstra virtual reality project simulates hurricane experience." *Newsday*, May 10, 2018. https://nwsdy.li/31GKuxa

Lozano, Juan, A., "One Year Post-Harvey, Recovery Toughest for the Poor." *Insurance Journal*, August 24, 2018. https://bit.ly/2LenrmL

MacMath, Jillian. "AccuWeather's 2019 Atlantic hurricane season forecast." AccuWeather, July 1, 2019. https://bit.ly/2YJE67M

Milman, Oliver. "How do cities rebuild after hurricanes like Harvey and Irma?" *The Guardian*, September 8, 2017. https://bit.ly/2vSUkAO

Poon, Linda. "Houston Looks for a Smarter, More Equitable Path to Hurricane Recovery." CityLab. October 22, 2018. https://bit.ly/2kplvP9

Resnick, Brian. "Another dangerous tropical cyclone just hit Mozambique." *Vox*, April 25, 2019. https://bit.ly/2Pv5WjW

Roberts, Patrick. "5 things that have changed about FEMA since Katrina – and 5 that haven't." *The Conversation*, September 25, 2017. https://bit.ly/2h5keuq

"Survey: One Year after Hurricane Harvey, 3 in 10 Affected Texas Gulf Coast Residents Say Their Lives Remain Disrupted." Episcopal Health Foundation, August 23, 2018. https://bit.ly/2MJNwwV

Wilkinson, Bard. "Design of cities must change to withstand 'category 6' mega storms." *CNN*, September 17, 2018. https://cnn.it/2Nidusp

Chapter 5

Pierre-Louis, Kendra. "There's actually no such thing as a natural disaster." *Popular Science*, October 2, 2017. http://bit.ly/2MjBpqu

"What Are Natural Hazards?" Organization of American States. http://bit.ly/2yWNvxc

Learning More

Books

Bell, Samantha S. *Detecting Hurricanes.* North Star Editions, 2017.

Challen, Paul. *Hurricane and Typhoon Alert.* Crabtree Publishing, 2004.

Elkins, Elizabeth. *Investigating Hurricanes.* Capstone Press, 2017.

Shofner, Melissa Raé. *Hammered by Hurricanes.* PowerKids Press, 2018.

Websites

Read hurricane safety tips from Weather Wiz Kids. **www.weatherwiz kids.com/weather-hurricane.htm**

Learn what hurricanes are from NASA experts. **https://go.nasa. gov/2krCu3i**

Discover how technology is used to track hurricanes. **https://bit.ly/2lXD6Oq**

Learn how satellites see through hurricanes. **https://bit.ly/2mk3tyc**

Glossary

absorb To soak up

aftermath The aftereffects of a major unpleasant event such as a natural disaster

aid agencies Groups that help people during disasters

atmospheric pressure The force pushing against objects from the weight of the air above them

building codes Rules and regulations that define how buildings are constructed safely

climate change Changing weather patterns over time generally considered to be caused by human activity such as fossil fuel use

data Information

deflect To cause something that is moving to change direction

erosion The gradual wearing away of something by natural forces such as water, wind, or ice

evacuating Removing from danger to a safer place

evaporating Turning from a liquid into a gas or vapor

ice sheets Very large and thick areas of ice that cover a region

infrastructure Things such as transportation, buildings, communications, and power supplies that a society needs to function

inland Toward the middle of a country, away from the coast

integrate To combine with or mix with

landfall Reaching land after traveling by sea or by air

levees Structures made of soil that are built to prevent the overflow of a river

nonperishable Able to be stored for a long time without rotting or spoiling

northern hemisphere The half of Earth that is north of the equator

practices Set ways of doing something

preparedness The state of being ready for something

radar A device that sends out radio waves for finding the position and speed of a moving object

risk The possibility that something bad will happen

simulation Processes made to look or act like something real

southern hemisphere The half of Earth that is south of the equator

torrential Fast-falling and heavy

United Nations An organization made up of 193 countries that works to promote peace and human rights around the world

updrafts Upward currents of air or other gas

vulnerable Easily hurt or damaged

weather balloons Scientific instruments that are used to collect information about atmospheric weather conditions

wind farms Groups of wind turbines in the same area

wind turbines Tall structures with large blades that are used to generate electricity

Index

About the Author

Rachel Seigel is an avid book enthusiast with more than 15 years of experience working with schools and libraries, matching books to readers. She is also the author of several nonfiction books for children. When she isn't writing or researching fun facts, she enjoys spending time with her boyfriend and her mischievous dog.